Python Programming
Beginner's Cookbook

JAE W. LEE

DEDICATION

To the budding chefs in the kitchen of coding, to those who are taking their first steps into the vast and flavorful world of Python programming, this book is for you. Just as a chef begins with understanding basic ingredients and simple recipes, you embark on a journey to master the ingredients of code and the recipes of software creation. Let each page be a steppingstone in your path to culinary mastery in the digital kitchen, where arrays and algorithms are your herbs and spices, and functions and loops become your essential cooking techniques. Do not fear the heat of challenges and errors; they are but the stoves and ovens that transform raw ideas into exquisite programs. Approach this adventure with the passion and curiosity of a chef exploring new cuisines, and let this guide be your cookbook, leading you from basic syntax to the crafting of intricate software dishes. May it inspire and equip you to cook up programs that delight, solve, and innovate. In the grand kitchen of programming, you have the potential to become a master chef, blending logic and creativity into code that tantalizes the palate of our digital world.

With belief in your potential,
Jae   W.   Lee

CONTENTS

PREFACE

Introduction to Python Programming

Hi there! You're about to start an awesome adventure into Python programming. Python is a super popular language because it's easy to learn and useful. It's used in lots of different areas like making websites, analyzing data, and even in science and tech stuff.

Why Python is Great

- Easy to Learn: Python is straightforward. It's like writing in English, which is perfect if you're just starting. You won't get lost in tricky code, so you can focus on learning how to program.
- Super Versatile: You can use Python for all sorts of things. Whether you want to automate simple tasks, build a website, or do cool data science projects, Python's got you covered.
- Lots of Help Available: Python has a huge community. This means you can find lots of guides, online forums, and extra resources to help you out.
- Good for Your Career: Knowing Python can open up many job opportunities. It's a skill that's really in demand in areas like web development and data analysis.

What You'll Learn in This Book

- Starting Simple: You'll begin with easy stuff like writing basic Python scripts, understanding variables, and knowing different types of data.
- Making Choices in Code: Learn how to make your programs make decisions using if-else statements and repeat tasks with loops.
- Organizing Data: Get to grips with lists and dictionaries which help you keep your data neat and useable.
- Reuse Your Code: Functions help you use the same code many times without rewriting it. You'll learn how to make and use them.
- Building with Classes: We'll show you how to use classes and objects, which are big parts of Python programming.

- Working with Files: Discover how to read and write files, a key skill for lots of programming jobs.
- Using Tools and Libraries: Learn how to add extra features to Python with modules and libraries.

Remember, learning programming is like learning a new language; it might seem hard at first, but with practice, you'll get better. This book is here to give you a strong start in Python programming with lots of practical examples and projects.

Ready to start coding in Python? Let's go!

How to Use This Book

This book is designed to guide you into the world of Python programming. To ensure that you get the most out of this book, there are a few important steps and recommendations on setting up your local environment and how to approach the content within these pages.

Setting Up Your Local Environment

Before you dive into the code examples and exercises in this book, it's essential to set up a local environment where you can write and run Python code. Here's what you need to do:

1. **Python Installation**: First and foremost, you'll need Python installed on your computer. If you haven't installed Python yet, don't worry! **The appendix of this book contains detailed instructions on how to install Python** for various operating systems, including Windows, macOS, and Linux.
2. **Choosing a Code Editor**: While Python comes with a basic editor called IDLE, you might find it more convenient to use a more advanced code editor. Some popular options include Visual Studio Code, PyCharm, and Sublime Text. These editors offer features like syntax highlighting and code completion that can make coding more accessible and enjoyable.
3. **Test Your Setup**: After installing Python and setting up your code editor, test your environment by running a simple Python script. For example, you can **write print("Hello, Python!") and run it** to see if you get the output correctly.

Approaching the Book

As you progress through the book, each chapter will introduce new concepts along with code examples and mini-projects. Here are some tips on how to approach them:

- **Read Actively**: As you read each chapter, type out and run the code examples in your code editor. This active participation will help you understand the concepts better.
- **Mini-Projects**: At the end of each chapter, you will find mini-projects designed to apply the concepts you've learned. Try to solve these projects on your own before looking at the provided solutions.
- **Practice Regularly**: Consistent practice is key to learning programming. Try to code every day, even if it's only for a short period.

By setting up your local environment and following these guidelines, you will be well-prepared to embark on your journey into Python programming. Remember, the path to becoming proficient in programming is a journey of continuous learning and practice.

CHAPTER 1

HELLO, WORLD! - A GENTLE INTRODUCTION TO PYTHON

Welcome to the exciting world of Python programming! As we embark on this journey together, let's start from the very basics to ensure a strong foundation.

1. The 'Hello World' Program

Our first step is the traditional 'Hello World' program. This program is a rite of passage for all new programmers. It's simple yet significant, teaching you the basics of syntax and output.

```Python
# Printing a string with print() function

print("Hello World")
```

- The `print( )` Function: This function is used to output text to the screen. In the example, `"Hello World"` is displayed.

- **Comments**: In Python, we use the `#` symbol to write comments. Comments are notes in your code that are not executed. They are essential for making your code understandable.

```Python
# This is a single-line comment


""" This is a multi-line comment

    spanning multiple lines """
```

2. Understanding Variables and Basic Operations

Before delving into operations, let's understand what variables are. Variables are like containers where we store data.

- **Variables**: Think of a variable as a box where you can store something, like a number or text. In programming, these "boxes" can store different types of data.
- **Data Types**: Python has various data types, including:
  - Integers (whole numbers like 3, -1)
  - Strings (text like "Hello")
  - Floating Point Numbers (numbers with decimal points like 3.14)

```Python
x = 15  # Integer

y = "Hello"  # String

z = 3.14  # Floating Point Number
```

- **Arithmetic Operations**: Python can perform basic math operations like addition (`+`), subtraction (`-`), multiplication (`*`), and division (`/`).

```Python
# Arithmetic Operations
a = 10
b = 5
sum = a + b  # Addition
difference = a - b  # Subtraction
product = a * b  # Multiplication
quotient = a / b  # Division
```

- **The Plus-Equals Operator (`+=`)**: This operator is a shortcut to add a value to a variable.

```Python
a += b  # Equivalent to a = a + b
```

- **The Modulo Operator (`%`)**: This operator finds the remainder in a division.

```Python
remainder = a % b
```

3. String Concatenation

As you learn, you'll encounter errors. Understanding them is key to becoming a proficient programmer.

- **ZeroDivisionError**: Occurs when you try to divide a number by zero.
- **NameError**: Happens when you try to use a variable that hasn't been defined.
- **SyntaxError**: These are grammatical errors in your code, like

missing a quote or a parenthesis.

```Python
# Handling Errors

# Uncomment below lines one at a time to see the errors

# print(10 / 0)  # ZeroDivisionError

# print(undefined_var)  # NameError

# print('Hello)  # SyntaxError
```

Remember, making mistakes is a part of learning. Each error is an opportunity to understand Python better. In the next chapter, we'll dive deeper into Python's world, exploring more complex concepts and building upon what we've learned here.

Code strong!

Mini Project 1: Personalized Greeting Generator

Problem Statement:

- Design a Python program that interacts with the user, asking for their name and the current time of day (morning, afternoon, evening). The program should then generate a personalized greeting based on the time of day.

Project Breakdown:

1. User Input: Collect the user's name and the current time of day.
2. Conditional Logic: Use if, elif, and else statements to tailor the greeting based on the time of day.
3. String Concatenation: Combine user input with a greeting message.
4. Error Handling: Include basic validation for time of day input.

Mini Project 2: Simple Arithmetic Quiz

Problem Statement:

- Create an interactive quiz that presents a simple arithmetic question (addition, subtraction, multiplication, division) to the user. The program should ask the user for the answer and provide feedback on whether they are correct or not.

Project Breakdown:

1. Generating a Question: Use basic arithmetic operations to generate a question.
2. User Input: Ask the user to input their answer.
3. Evaluation: Check if the user's answer is correct.
4. Feedback: Inform the user whether their answer is correct or incorrect.

CHAPTER 2

CONTROL FLOW - DIRECTING YOUR PROGRAM'S PATH

Control flow is the backbone of programming logic. It's how your program makes decisions and follows specific paths based on certain conditions. This episode introduces you to the fundamental concepts of control flow in Python.

1. Conditional Statements: if, elif, and else

- What are Conditional Statements?: These are instructions that execute different blocks of code depending on certain conditions.
- **The `if` Statement**: Used to test a specific condition. If the condition is `True`, the indented code block under it runs.
- **The `elif` (else if) Statement**: Used to test additional conditions if the previous `if` or `elif` conditions are `False`.
- **The `else` Statement**: Runs if all the `if` and `elif` conditions above it are `False`.

```python
Python
number = 10

if number > 0:

    print("Positive number")

elif number == 0:

    print("Zero")

else:

    print("Negative number")
```

2. Comparison Operators

- Purpose: These operators are used to compare values.
- `==` **Operator**: Checks if two values are equal.
- `!=` **Operator**: Checks if two values are not equal.

```python
Python
# Comparison Operators

print(number == 10)  # Checks if number is equal to 10

print(number != 5)   # Checks if number is not equal to 5
```

3. Logical Operators: and, or, not

- Combining Conditions: Logical operators allow you to combine or modify conditions.
- `and` **Operator**: Returns `True` if both conditions are true.
- `or` **Operator**: Returns `True` if at least one of the conditions is true.
- `not` **Operator**: Inverts the truth value of the condition.

```python
Python
is_sunny = True

is_raining = False


# Using 'and' and 'not'

if is_sunny and not is_raining:

    print("It's a sunny day")


# Using 'or'

if is_sunny or is_raining:

    print("It might be a rainbow day")
```

4. Boolean Values: True and False

- Boolean Basics: Booleans represent one of two values: `True` or `False`.
- Using Booleans: These are often used in conditional statements to represent conditions.

```python
Python
is_open = True

is_closed = not is_open
```

Understanding control flow is crucial as it lets you control the decision-making process in your programs. It's what makes your code "smart" and able to respond differently under varying conditions. In the next episode, we'll explore Lists, another fundamental concept in Python programming.

Code strong!

Mini Project 3: Weather Activity Adviser

Problem Statement:

- Create a Python program that recommends activities to users based on weather conditions. The user should input the weather (sunny, rainy, or snowy), and the program should suggest suitable activities.

Project Breakdown:

1. User Input: Ask the user to input the current weather condition.
2. Conditional Logic: Use if, elif, and else statements to decide on activities based on the weather input.
3. Output: Display the activity recommendation.

Mini Project 4: Simple Authentication System

Problem Statement:

- Develop a basic authentication system where a user can input a username and password. The program should verify if the entered credentials match predefined ones and respond accordingly.

Project Breakdown:

1. User Input: Prompt for username and password.
2. Verification: Compare input with predefined credentials.
3. Logical Operators: Use logical operators to determine if both username and password are correct.
4. Output: Inform the user whether they are authenticated or not.

CHAPTER 3

LISTS - ORGANIZING YOUR DATA

Control flow is the backbone of programming logic. It's how your program makes decisions and follows specific paths based on certain conditions. This episode introduces you to the fundamental concepts of control flow in Python.

1. Basics of Lists

- What is a List?: A list in Python is like a container that holds a collection of items. These items can be of any data type, and a single list can contain a mix of different types.
- Creating a List: Lists are created by enclosing items in square brackets `[ ]`.

```python
fruits = ["apple", "banana", "cherry"]
vegetables = ["spinach", "kale", "carrot"]
```

2. Concatenating Lists

- Combining Lists: You can combine two lists simply by using the `+` operator.

```Python
food = fruits + vegetables
```

3. List Methods

- Adding Items: The `.append( )` method adds an item to the end of the list.
- Removing Items: The `.remove( )` method removes a specific item from the list.
- Counting Items: The `.count( )` method counts the number of times an item appears in the list.
- Sorting Items: The `.sort( )` method sorts the items in the list.

```Python
fruits.append("orange")

fruits.remove("banana")

print(fruits.count("apple"))

fruits.sort()
```

4. Indexing and Slicing

- Zero-Based Indexing: Lists are indexed starting from 0. The first item is at index 0, the second at index 1, and so on.
- Negative Indexing: Negative indices count from the end of the list, with `-1` being the last item.
- Slicing Lists: Slicing allows you to create a sublist by specifying a start and end index.

```python
first_fruit = fruits[0]

last_vegetable = vegetables[-1]

slice_fruits = fruits[1:3]
```

5. Advanced List Operations

- Nested Lists: Lists can contain other lists. This is used to create 2D lists or matrices.
- Length of a List: The `len( )` function returns the number of items in a list.
- Inserting and Removing at Specific Positions: The `.insert( )` method adds an item at a specified index, and `.pop( )` removes the item at a specific index.

```python
matrix = [[1, 2], [3, 4]]

matrix[0][1] = 10

print(len(fruits))

sorted_vegetables = sorted(vegetables)

fruits.insert(1, "mango")

popped_fruit = fruits.pop()
```

Through this chapter, you will learn how to effectively manage and manipulate lists, a crucial skill in Python programming. Lists are fundamental to organizing data in Python, and understanding them will greatly enhance your ability to write effective and efficient code. In the next chapter, we dive into the world of loops, another cornerstone of programming.

Code strong!

Mini Project 5: Recipe Ingredient Organizer

Problem Statement:

- Develop a Python program that helps users organize ingredients for a recipe. The user should be able to add, remove, and view ingredients in a list. Additionally, they should be able to sort the list alphabetically and view the total number of ingredients.

Project Breakdown:

1. Creating and Managing a List: Use a list to store ingredients.
2. Adding and Removing Ingredients: Implement list methods `.append()`, `.remove()`, and `.insert()`.
3. Sorting and Counting: Use `.sort()` for sorting and `len()` for counting ingredients.
4. User Interaction: Allow users to choose actions (add, remove, sort, view, count) in a loop.

Mini Project 6: Personal Library Catalog

Problem Statement:

- Create a program that manages a personal library catalog. The user should be able to add books with title and author, view the entire catalog, and search for books by title.

Project Breakdown:

1. Nested Lists: Utilize nested lists to store book information (title and author).
2. Adding Books: Implement functionality to add new books to the library.
3. Viewing Catalog: Allow users to view all books in the catalog.
4. Searching for Books: Implement a search feature to find books by title.

CHAPTER 4

LOOPS - MASTERING REPETITION

Loops are a fundamental concept in programming that allow us to execute a block of code multiple times. This chapter introduces you to different types of loops in Python and how to control their behavior.

1. The for Loop

Purpose: The `for` loop is used to iterate over a sequence, like a list, a tuple, a dictionary, a set, or a string.

Using `range( )`: The `range( )` function is often used with `for` loops to specify the number of iterations.

```Python
for i in range(5):
    print(i)
```

2. The while Loop

- How It Works: A `while` loop repeatedly executes as long as a given condition is true.
- Incrementing Variables: Inside the `while` loop, it's common to modify a variable to eventually make the condition false and end the loop.

```python
count = 0

while count < 5:

    print(count)

    count += 1
```

3. Controlling Loop Execution

- `break` Keyword: Used to exit a loop prematurely.
- `continue` Keyword: Skips the current iteration and continues with the next one.

```python
for num in range(10):

    if num == 5:

        break

    if num % 2 == 0:

        continue

    print(num)
```

4. List Comprehensions

- Efficiency: A list comprehension provides a concise way to create lists.
- Syntax: It consists of brackets containing an expression followed by a `for` clause.

```python
Python
squares = [x**2 for x in range(10)]
```

5. Nested Loops

- Concept: A loop inside another loop. Nested loops are useful for working with multidimensional data.
- Example Usage: Commonly used in scenarios like accessing elements of a matrix.

```python
Python
for x in range(3):

    for y in range(3):

        print(f"({x}, {y})")
```

6. Caution with Infinite Loops

- Infinite Loops: A loop that has no end. It's important to be cautious with conditions that never become false.
- Usage: Typically used intentionally in certain situations, but can also be a result of a programming error.

```
Python
# Example of an infinite loop

# Uncomment with caution

# while True:

#    print("Infinite loop")
```

By mastering loops, you will significantly enhance your ability to write dynamic and efficient Python programs. This chapter provides a solid foundation for using loops to automate repetitive tasks and handle data more effectively. In the next chapter, we will explore functions, a powerful tool for creating reusable and organized code.

Code strong!

Mini Project 7: Multiplication Table Generator

Problem Statement:

- Create a program that generates and prints a multiplication table for numbers up to a user-specified limit. The table should be formatted in a readable manner.

Project Breakdown:

1. User Input for Limit: Use a for loop to iterate over a range of numbers.
2. Generating Multiplication Table: Utilize nested for loops to calculate and print the multiplication table.
3. Formatting Output: Ensure the table is well-formatted for readability.

Mini Project 8: Prime Number Finder

Problem Statement:

- Develop a program that finds and displays all prime numbers up to a specified limit. Include functionality to skip even numbers for efficiency.

Project Breakdown:

1. User Input for Limit: Prompt the user for the upper limit of prime numbers.
2. Finding Prime Numbers: Use a `while` loop with nested `for` loops to check for prime numbers.
3. Optimization with `continue`: Skip even numbers (except 2) for efficiency.
4. Output: Display   all   the   prime   numbers   found.

CHAPTER 5

FUNCTIONS - BUILDING BLOCKS OF CODE

Functions are a cornerstone of Python programming, allowing you to organize and reuse code effectively. They help in making your code modular and manageable. In this chapter, we will explore how to define, use, and understand functions in Python.

1. Defining Functions

- Basic Structure: Functions are defined using the `def` keyword, followed by the function name and parentheses containing any parameters.
- Purpose: Each function is designed to perform a specific task.

```python
Python
def greet(name):
    return f"Hello, {name}!"
```

2. Calling Functions

- Executing Functions: To execute a function, you call it by its name followed by parentheses containing any arguments.
- Arguments vs. Parameters: Arguments are the actual values you pass to the function; parameters are the variables that receive these values.

```python
Python
print(greet("Alice"))
```

3. Functions with Multiple Parameters

- Multiple Inputs: Functions can accept more than one parameter, allowing them to work with multiple pieces of data.

```python
Python
def add(a, b):
    return a + b
```

4. Keyword Arguments

- Specifying Arguments by Name: Keyword arguments are a way to pass arguments to a function by explicitly naming each parameter.
- Clarity and Flexibility: This approach can make the function calls clearer and more flexible.

```python
Python
def full_name(first, last):

    return first + " " + last



print(full_name(first="Alice", last="Smith"))
```

5. Returning Multiple Values

- Multiple Outputs: Functions in Python can return more than one value, separated by commas.
- Unpacking Values: The returned values can be unpacked into individual variables.

```python
Python
def arithmetic_ops(a, b):

    return a + b, a - b, a * b, a / b



sum, difference, product, quotient = arithmetic_ops(10, 5)

print("Sum:", sum, "Difference:", difference)
```

6. Understanding Scope

- Local vs. Global Variables: Variables defined within a function are local to that function. Variables defined outside of any function are global.
- Scope Importance: Understanding scope is crucial for managing variables and avoiding conflicts in your program.

```Python
global_var = "Global"


def test_scope():

  local_var = "Local"

  print(local_var)


test_scope()

print(global_var)
```

Functions are powerful tools in Python, enabling you to write efficient and reusable code. They form the building blocks of larger programs, making your code organized and scalable. In the next chapter, we will delve into the world of strings, exploring how to manipulate and work with textual data in Python.

Code strong!

Mini Project 9: Unit Converter

Problem Statement:

- Create a Python program that converts units between kilometers and miles. The user should be able to choose the type of conversion and then input a value, which will be converted accordingly.

Project Breakdown:

1. Defining Functions: Create functions for converting kilometers to miles and vice versa.

2. User Interaction: Allow the user to choose the type of conversion and enter the value.

3. Processing Input: Use the appropriate function based on the user's choice to perform the conversion.

4. Displaying Output: Show the converted value to the user.

Mini Project 10: Simple Calculator with Memory

Problem Statement:

- Build a simple calculator that can perform addition, subtraction, multiplication, and division. The calculator should also maintain a history of the last operation performed, which can be viewed by the user.

Project Breakdown:

1. Defining Functions: Create functions for each arithmetic operation and a function to display the last operation.
2. Storing Last Operation: Keep track of the last operation performed.
3. User Interaction: Allow users to choose an operation and input values.
4. Displaying History: Include an option to view the last operation performed.

CHAPTER 6

STRINGS - CRAFTING TEXTUAL DATA

Strings are a fundamental part of programming in Python, used extensively to represent and manipulate textual data. This chapter delves into various operations and methods you can perform with strings, enhancing your ability to handle text in Python.

1. Basic String Operations

- Introduction to Strings: Strings are sequences of characters enclosed in quotes. They can be manipulated and modified using various methods.
- String Methods: Python provides a variety of string methods for common tasks.
    - `.lower( )`: Converts a string to lowercase.
    - `.upper( )`: Converts a string to uppercase.
    - `.split( )`: Splits a string into a list of substrings.

```
Python
phrase = "Hello, World!"

print(phrase.lower())

print(phrase.upper())

print(phrase.split(','))
```

2. String Formatting

- Dynamic Text: The `.format( )` method allows you to insert values into a string, making your output dynamic and flexible.

```
Python
formatted_string = "Welcome, {}".format("Alice")

print(formatted_string)
```

3. Accessing and Extracting Parts of Strings

- Indexing and Slicing: Strings in Python are indexed, allowing you to access individual characters or a range of characters.
  - o Indexing: Retrieves a single character.
  - o Slicing: Retrieves a substring.

```
Python
print(phrase[0])

print(phrase[1:5])
```

4. Iterating Through Strings

- Using Loops: You can iterate through each character in a string using a loop.

```
Python
for char in phrase:

    print(char)
```

5. Replacing Substrings

- Modification: The `.replace( )` method allows you to replace parts of the string with different text.

```
Python
replaced_string = phrase.replace("World", "Python")

print(replaced_string)
```

6. Checking Substring Existence

- `in` Syntax: You can check if a specific sequence of characters exists within a string.

```
Python
if "Hello" in phrase:

    print("Hello is in the phrase")
```

7. Escaping Characters

- Special Characters: Sometimes, you need to include special characters in a string, like quotes. The backslash (`\`) is used to escape characters.

```
Python
escaped_string = "He said, \"Python is awesome!\""

print(escaped_string)
```

Strings are incredibly versatile in Python, and mastering their manipulation is crucial for any Python programmer. This chapter has equipped you with the knowledge to effectively work with strings, opening up a wide array of possibilities for text processing and manipulation. In the next chapter, we will explore modules, a key feature in Python that allows you to expand your programming horizons.

Code strong!

Mini Project 11: Personalized Story Creator

Problem Statement:

- Develop a Python program that creates a personalized story for the user. The program should ask for the user's name, a favorite color, and a hobby. It should then generate a short story incorporating these details.

Project Breakdown:

1. User Input: Collect the user's name, favorite color, and hobby.

2. String Formatting: Use the `.format( )` method to dynamically insert these details into a pre-defined story.

3. Output: Display the personalized story.

Mini Project 12: Palindrome Checker

Problem Statement:

- Create a Python program that checks if a given string is a palindrome (a word, phrase, or sequence that reads the same backward as forward). The program should ignore spaces and be case-insensitive.

Project Breakdown:

1. User Input: Prompt the user to enter a string.
2. String Manipulation: Convert the string to a standardized format (e.g., lowercase, remove spaces) for easy comparison.
3. Palindrome Check: Determine if the string is a palindrome.
4. Output: Inform the user whether the entered string is a palindrome.

CHAPTER 7

MODULES - EXPANDING YOUR TOOLBOX

Modules in Python are akin to toolboxes. They are collections of functions and methods that can be imported into your programs, providing additional functionality not built into the core language. This chapter will introduce you to Python modules, show you how to import and use them, and guide you through some common modules that are incredibly useful in everyday programming.

1. Understanding Modules

- What Are Modules?: Modules are files containing Python definitions and statements. They extend the capabilities of Python.
- Importing Modules: To use a module, you must first `import` it into your program.

2. Importing and Using Modules

- The `import` Statement: This is how you bring a module into your script.
- Accessing Module Functions: Once imported, you can access

functions and variables defined in the module.

```python
import random

import datetime
```

3. Working with the datetime Module

- Purpose: The `datetime` module is used for manipulating dates and times.
- Using `datetime`: You can perform a variety of operations related to time, such as getting the current date and time.

```python
current_time = datetime.datetime.now()

print(current_time)
```

4. Aliasing Modules

- The `as` Keyword: You can create an alias for a module for easier and shorter reference.
- Advantages of Aliasing: This makes your code more readable and allows you to avoid naming conflicts.

```python
import math as m

print(m.sqrt(16))
```

5. The random Module

- Random Number Generation: The `random` module is used for generating random numbers and choosing random elements from a list.

- Functions in `random`: This module provides various functions like `randint( )` for random integers and `choice( )` for selecting a random item from a sequence.

```Python
print(random.randint(1, 10))

print(random.choice(['apple', 'banana', 'cherry']))
```

By the end of this chapter, you will have a solid understanding of how to incorporate modules into your Python scripts to leverage their powerful features. Modules are essential in Python programming, enabling you to expand the capabilities of your programs significantly. In the next chapter, we'll explore dictionaries, a powerful data type for storing and organizing data in key-value pairs.

Code strong!

Mini Project 13: Personal Event Countdown

Problem Statement:

- Design a Python program that counts down to a specific date provided by the user (e.g., birthday, holiday, appointment). The program should display the number of days remaining until the event.

Project Breakdown:

1. Using the datetime Module: Import and use the datetime module to handle dates.
2. User Input for Event Date: Prompt the user to enter the date of their event.
3. Calculating Days Remaining: Determine the difference between the current date and the event date.
4. Output: Display the number of days left until the event.

Mini Project 14: Random Inspirational Quote Generator

Problem Statement:

- Create a Python program that randomly selects and displays an inspirational quote from a predefined list each time it is run.

Project Breakdown:

1. Using the random Module: Utilize the random module to select a random quote.
2. List of Quotes: Define a list containing several inspirational quotes.
3. Random Selection: Use `random.choice( )` to select a quote from the list.
4. Output: Print the randomly selected inspirational quote.

CHAPTER 8

DICTIONARIES - MAPPING YOUR DATA

Dictionaries in Python are incredibly versatile and powerful, providing a means of storing data in a key-value pair format. This chapter will guide you through the essentials of using dictionaries, showing you how they can be used to store and organize complex data efficiently.

1. Understanding Dictionaries

- Definition: A dictionary in Python is a collection of key-value pairs. Each key is unique and is used to access its corresponding value.
- Flexibility: Unlike lists, dictionaries do not maintain order. Instead, they are optimized for retrieving data using keys.

2. Creating and Accessing Dictionaries

- Creating a Dictionary: Dictionaries are created with curly braces `{ }` with pairs separated by commas.
- Accessing Data: Values are accessed by specifying their key in square brackets `[ ]`.

```python
Python
person = {"name": "Alice", "age": 30}
print(person["name"])
```

3. Modifying Dictionaries

- Adding Entries: You can add new key-value pairs simply by assigning a value to a new key.
- Modifying Values: Values can be updated by reassigning a new value to an existing key.

```python
Python
person["gender"] = "Female"
person["name"] = "Bob"
```

4. Dictionary Methods

- Using `.get( )`: Safely access values, returning `None` if the key is not found.
- Removing Entries with `.pop( )`: Removes a key-value pair and returns the value.

```python
Python
print(person.get("age"))
person.pop("gender")
```

5. Merging Dictionaries

- The `.update( )` Method: Merge two dictionaries, where the second dictionary's key-value pairs are added to the first.

```python
Python
additional_info = {"hobby": "painting", "city": "New York"}

person.update(additional_info)
```

6. Versatility of Dictionary Values

- Holding Various Data Types: Dictionary values can be strings, numbers, lists, or even other dictionaries, making them suitable for structuring complex data.

Dictionaries are key to managing structured data in Python. They offer a fast and intuitive way to associate keys with values, making data retrieval simple and efficient. By the end of this chapter, you will have a thorough understanding of how to use dictionaries for various data storage and manipulation tasks. In the next chapter, we will explore how to interact with files, enabling your programs to read and write data to external sources.

Code strong!

Mini Project 15: Personal Contact Book

Problem Statement:

- Develop a Python program that acts as a personal contact book. The user should be able to add, remove, and search for contacts (name, phone number, and email address) using a dictionary.

Project Breakdown:

- Creating and Managing a Dictionary: Use a dictionary to store contact information.
- Adding and Removing Contacts: Implement functionality to add or remove a contact.
- Searching for Contacts: Allow users to search for a contact by name.
- User Interaction: Create a menu-driven interface for interaction.

Mini Project 16: Vocabulary Builder

Problem Statement:

- Create a program that helps users build their vocabulary. The user can add new words along with their meanings to a dictionary. The program should allow the user to view all added words and their meanings, and search for specific words.

Project Breakdown:

- Dictionary for Storing Words and Meanings: Use a dictionary to hold word-meaning pairs.
- Adding New Words: Implement a feature to add new words and their meanings.
- Viewing and Searching Words: Allow users to view all words or search for specific words.
- User Interface: Develop a simple menu-driven interface for interaction.

CHAPTER 9

FILES - HANDLING EXTERNAL DATA

Interacting with files is a fundamental aspect of programming in Python, enabling you to store and retrieve data from your computer. This chapter will cover the essentials of file operations, including reading, writing, and appending data to files. We'll also delve into handling popular data formats like CSV and JSON.

1. Fundamentals of File Operations

- Understanding File Objects: A file object in Python acts as a bridge between your program and a file on your computer.
- Opening and Closing Files: The `open( )` function is used to open a file, and it's crucial to close it properly to free up system resources.

2. Reading from Files

- Reading Entire Content: The `.read( )` method reads the entire content of the file.
- Reading Line by Line: The `.readline( )` and `.readlines( )`

methods are used to read files line by line or to get all lines as a list, respectively.

```python
with open('sample.txt', 'r') as file:
    content = file.read()
    print(content)
```

3. Writing and Appending to Files

- Writing Data: The `.write( )` method is used to write data to a file.
- Appending Data: Opening a file in append mode (`'a'`) allows you to add data to the end of the file without overwriting existing content.

```python
with open('sample_write.txt', 'w') as file:
    file.write("Hello, Python!")

with open('sample_append.txt', 'a') as file:
    file.write("\nAdding a new line")
```

4. Working with JSON Data

- JSON in Python: JSON (JavaScript Object Notation) is a popular format for data interchange. Python's `json` module allows you to parse JSON data easily.
- Reading and Writing JSON: Convert JSON data into Python dictionaries and vice versa using `json.load( )` and `json.dump( )`.

```python
Python
import json

with open('data.json', 'r') as file:

    data = json.load(file)

    print(data)


with open('data_write.json', 'w') as file:

    json.dump({"key": "value"}, file)
```

5. Handling CSV Files

- CSV File Operations: We'll briefly explore how to handle CSV (Comma-Separated Values) files, a common format for storing tabular data.

By the end of this chapter, you'll have a thorough understanding of file operations in Python, equipping you with the skills to read from and write to different types of files. This knowledge is crucial for any Python programmer, as it allows your programs to interact with a vast amount of external data. In the next chapter, we will dive into object-oriented programming with Python classes, an essential concept for building more complex and organized programs.

Code strong!

Mini Project 17: Personal Diary Application

Problem Statement:

- Develop a Python program that allows users to keep a digital diary. Users should be able to add new diary entries with the current date and time, view all entries, and append additional text to existing entries.

Project Breakdown:

1. Writing and Appending Diary Entries: Implement file operations to write and append diary entries.
2. Reading Entries: Use file reading methods to display all diary entries.
3. Date and Time Stamping: Utilize the datetime module to automatically add the date and time to each entry.
4. User Interface: Create a menu-driven interface to interact with the diary.

Mini Project 18: Contact List Manager

Problem Statement:

- Create a Python program to manage a contact list. The application should enable users to add new contacts, update existing contacts, and store the contact list in a JSON file. Contacts should include a name, phone number, and email address.

Project Breakdown:

1. JSON for Data Storage: Use JSON format to store and retrieve contact information.
2. Adding and Updating Contacts: Implement functions to add and update contacts in the JSON file.
3. Reading Contacts from File: Enable users to view all contacts stored in the JSON file.
4. User Interface: Develop a menu-driven user interface for interaction.

CHAPTER 10

CLASSES - BLUEPRINT OF OBJECTS

Welcome to the exciting finale of our Python programming journey! This chapter introduces you to the concept of classes and object-oriented programming, a fundamental aspect of Python. Classes are essentially blueprints for creating objects, providing structure and functionality to your code.

1. Introduction to Classes

- What is a Class?: A class in Python is a blueprint for creating objects. It defines a set of attributes and methods that characterize any object of the class.
- Defining a Class: Classes are defined using the `class` keyword.

2. The init Method and Object Initialization

- Creating Objects: An object is an instance of a class. The `__init__` method, known as the initializer, sets up an object's initial state by assigning values to object attributes.
- Self Parameter: The `self` parameter in methods refers to the

instance calling the method.

```python
class Person:

    def __init__(self, name, age):

        self.name = name

        self.age = age
```

3. Methods and Object Behavior

- Defining Methods: Methods are functions defined inside a class that describe the behaviors of an object.
- Accessing Methods: You can call a method on an object to perform operations or actions.

```python
alice = Person("Alice", 30)

print(alice.greet())
```

4. Static Methods

- Using **@staticmethod**: This decorator indicates that a method belongs to the class as a whole and not to a particular instance.
- Class-wide Operations: Static methods are used for operations that don't require access to an instance's attributes.

```python
Python
class Math:

  @staticmethod

  def add(a, b):

    return a + b


print(Math.add(10, 5))
```

5. The **repr** Method

- Object Representation: The `__repr__` method is used to provide a string representation of an object, helpful for debugging.
- Customizing Representation: You can define how your object should be represented as a string.

```python
Python
class Circle:
  def __init__(self, radius):

    self.radius = radius


  def __repr__(self):

    return f"Circle with radius {self.radius}"
```

6. Exploring Objects with type( ) and dir( )

- Inspecting Objects: Use the `type( )` function to find an object's class and `dir( )` to discover its attributes and methods.

```python
Python
class Animal:
    def __init__(self, species):
        self.species = species

    def make_sound(self):
        print("Some generic animal sound")

# Creating an instance of Animal
my_pet = Animal("Dog")

# Using type()
print("The type of my_pet is:", type(my_pet))

# Using dir()
print("\nAttributes and methods of my_pet:")
print(dir(my_pet))
```

In this example, we define a class `Animal`, then create an instance named `my_pet`. The `type(my_pet)` reveals that `my_pet` is an instance of the `Animal` class. `dir(my_pet)` lists all the attributes and methods associated with this instance, giving you insight into what you can do with `my_pet`.

7. The **main** Block

- Entry Point of a Script: The `__main__` block is where a Python script starts execution. It's commonly used to organize code.

```Python
def greet(name):
  return f"Hello, {name}!"

def main():
    user_name = input("Enter your name: ")
    print(greet(user_name))

# Checking if the script is run directly
if __name__ == "__main__":
  main()
```

Here, we define a `greet` function and a `main` function. The `main` function calls `greet` after getting the user's name. The last part of the code checks if the script is being run directly (not imported as a module in another script). If it is, `main( )` is called. This approach keeps the flow of the script clear and helps in testing individual parts of the code.

By the end of this chapter, you'll have a comprehensive understanding of how classes and objects work in Python. This knowledge is crucial for building more complex, scalable, and organized programs. You're now well-equipped to continue exploring the vast and exciting world of Python programming.

Code strong!

Mini Project 19: Simple Bank Account Manager

Problem Statement:

- Create a Python program that simulates a simple bank account. Users should be able to create an account with a balance, deposit money, withdraw money, and check their balance. Implement these functionalities using classes and objects.

Project Breakdown:

1. Defining the Bank Account Class: Include methods for depositing, withdrawing, and checking balance.
2. Object Initialization: Use the __init__ method to initialize account details.
3. User Interaction: Allow users to perform banking operations through a menu-driven interface.
4. Error Handling: Include checks for invalid operations like withdrawing more than the balance.

Mini Project 20: Library Management System

Problem Statement:

- Develop a Python program to manage a library system. The system should allow adding books, viewing available books, and borrowing books. Implement these functionalities using classes and objects.

Project Breakdown:

1. Defining Library and Book Classes: Use classes to represent the library and books.
2. Methods for Library Operations: Include methods for adding, viewing, and borrowing books.
3. Tracking Borrowed Books: Maintain a list of borrowed books.
4. User Interface: Create a user interface for library operations.

CONCLUSION

As we wrap up this book, "Python Programming Beginner's Cookbook," I want to give you a big thumbs up for diving into Python programming. It's a big deal, and you did it! We started from scratch with the simple 'Hello, World!' and worked our way up to the cool stuff like classes and handling files. You've got the basics down, like controlling how your program runs, sorting your data in lists and dictionaries, making code you can use again with functions, and working with text using strings. Plus, we checked out how to use extra tools with modules and got a taste of object-oriented programming.

But hey, there's more out there to learn. If you want to build bigger programs and get into the nitty-gritty of designing software, there's a bunch more to explore. Things like advanced ways to organize data, algorithms, design patterns, web stuff with Django or Flask, and data science tools are your next steps. This stuff helps you build bigger, sophisticated programs and understand how big scale software is put together.

Remember, everyone starts at the beginning. Learning is a never-ending adventure that's super exciting. Be proud of how far you've come and keep that curiosity burning. Python's a big world that keeps growing, and it's full of chances for you to discover new things. Keep on coding, keep on learning, and most importantly, have fun on this journey. Keep coding strong, and let your love for programming take you to awesome places!

Jae W. Lee

APPENDIX

Python Installation Guide

Setting up Python on your computer is the first step in your programming journey. This guide will walk you through the process of installing Python on Windows, macOS, and Linux systems. Python's ease of installation is one of its strengths, so let's get started!

For Windows Users:

Download Python:

- Visit the official Python website at https://python.org
- Navigate to the Downloads section and choose the latest Python version for Windows.
- Click on the installer link to download the executable file.

Run the Installer:

- Locate the downloaded file and double-click to run the installer.
- Ensure you check the box that says "Add Python 3.x to PATH" before clicking "Install Now".
- Follow the on-screen instructions to complete the installation.

Verify the Installation:

- Open Command Prompt and type **python --version**
- If Python is installed correctly, you should see the version number.

For macOS Users:

Download Python:

- Go to https://python.org
- Head to the Downloads section and select the latest Python version for macOS.
- Download the macOS installer

Install Python:

- Open the downloaded package and follow the instructions to install Python.
- During installation, macOS might prompt you for your admin password.

Verify the Installation:

- Open Terminal and type **python3 –version**
- The installed Python version should be displayed.

For Linux Users:

Python usually comes pre-installed on many Linux distributions. To check if it's installed and to find out the version, follow these steps:

- Open Terminal.
- Type **python3 --version** or **python --version**

If Python is not installed or you need a different version, you can install it using your distribution's package manager. For Ubuntu, this would typically be:

- Update package lists: **sudo apt update**
- Install Python 3: **sudo apt install python3**

Post-Installation Steps:

- Install a Code Editor: While Python comes with IDLE, you might want to install a more feature-rich code editor like Visual Studio Code or PyCharm for a better coding experience.
- Update pip: **pip** is Python's package installer. Ensure it's up-to-date by running **python -m pip install --upgrade pip** in your command line or terminal.
- Explore Python: Try running a simple print statement like **print("Hello, Python!")** to see Python in action.

APPENDIX

Solutions to Mini Projects

Mini Project 1 Sample Code:

```python
# Personalized Greeting Generator

# User input for name and time of day
name = input("What is your name? ")
time_of_day = input("What is the current time of day (morning, afternoon, evening)? ").lower()

# Conditional logic for generating the greeting
if time_of_day == "morning":
    greeting = "Good morning"
elif time_of_day == "afternoon":
    greeting = "Good afternoon"
elif time_of_day == "evening":
    greeting = "Good evening"
else:
    greeting = "Hello"

# Outputting the personalized greeting
print(f"{greeting}, {name}!")
```

Explanation:
- The program requests the user's name and the current time of day.
- Based on the time of day, it selects an appropriate greeting.
- The final message is a combination of the selected greeting and the user's name.

Mini Project 2 Sample Code:

```python
# Simple Arithmetic Quiz

import random

# Generating two random numbers and an operation
num1 = random.randint(1, 10)
num2 = random.randint(1, 10)
operation = random.choice(["+", "-", "*", "/"])
question = f"What is {num1} {operation} {num2}?"

# Calculating the correct answer
if operation == "+":
    correct_answer = num1 + num2
elif operation == "-":
    correct_answer = num1 - num2
elif operation == "*":
    correct_answer = num1 * num2
elif operation == "/":
    correct_answer = round(num1 / num2, 2)

# Asking the user the question
print(question)
user_answer = float(input("Your answer: "))

# Providing feedback
if user_answer == correct_answer:
    print("Correct!")
else:
    print(f"Incorrect. The correct answer is {correct_answer}.")
```

Explanation:

- The program generates a random arithmetic question using two random numbers and a randomly chosen operation.

- It calculates the correct answer and rounds it to two decimal places for division.
- The user is then asked the question and inputs their answer.
- The program compares the user's answer to the correct answer and provides appropriate feedback.

Mini Project 3 Sample Code:

```Python
# Weather Activity Adviser

# User input for current weather
current_weather = input("Enter the current weather (sunny, rainy, snowy): ").lower()

# Conditional logic for activity suggestion
if current_weather == "sunny":
    activity = "It's a great day for a walk or a picnic!"
elif current_weather == "rainy":
    activity = "How about reading a book or watching a movie indoors?"
elif current_weather == "snowy":
    activity = "Perfect time for building a snowman or indoor baking!"
else:
    activity = "Hmm, not sure about that weather. Maybe enjoy some indoor activities!"

# Outputting the activity suggestion
print(activity)
```

Explanation:
- The program starts by asking the user to input the current weather condition.
- Based on the input, it uses `if`, `elif`, and `else` statements to suggest an appropriate activity.
- Finally, it prints the suggested activity.

Mini Project 4 Sample Code:

```python
Python
# Simple Authentication System

# Predefined credentials
correct_username = "user123"
correct_password = "pass321"

# User input for credentials
input_username = input("Enter your username: ")
input_password = input("Enter your password: ")

# Verification and output
if input_username == correct_username and input_password == correct_password:
    print("Authentication successful! Welcome!")
else:
    print("Authentication failed. Please check your username and password.")
```

Explanation:
- The program sets predefined username and password values.
- It then prompts the user for their username and password.
- Using the `and` logical operator, it checks if both entered username and password match the predefined ones.
- Finally, it prints a message indicating whether authentication was successful or not.

Mini Project 5 Sample Code:

```python
# Recipe Ingredient Organizer

# List to store ingredients
ingredients = []

while True:
    # User menu
    action = input("Choose an action (add, remove, sort, view, count, exit): ").lower()

    # Adding an ingredient
    if action == "add":
        item = input("Enter an ingredient to add: ")
        ingredients.append(item)

    # Removing an ingredient
    elif action == "remove":
        item = input("Enter an ingredient to remove: ")
        if item in ingredients:
            ingredients.remove(item)
        else:
            print("Ingredient not found.")

    # Sorting ingredients
    elif action == "sort":
        ingredients.sort()

    # Viewing ingredients
    elif action == "view":
        print("Ingredients:", ingredients)
```

```python
# Counting ingredients
elif action == "count":
    print("Total ingredients:", len(ingredients))

# Exiting the program
elif action == "exit":
    break

else:
    print("Invalid action. Please try again.")
```

Explanation:

- The program uses a while loop for continuous user interaction until 'exit' is chosen.
- The user can add or remove ingredients, which are managed using list methods.
- Sorting and counting functionalities provide additional utility.
- The program handles user inputs and provides appropriate feedback.

Mini Project 6 Sample Code:

```python
# Personal Library Catalog

# Library list
library = []

while True:
    # User menu
    action = input("Choose an action (add, view, search, exit): ").lower()

    # Adding a book
    if action == "add":
        title = input("Enter the book title: ")
        author = input("Enter the author's name: ")
        library.append([title, author])

    # Viewing the library
    elif action == "view":
        for book in library:
            print(f"Title: {book[0]}, Author: {book[1]}")

    # Searching for a book
    elif action == "search":
        search_title = input("Enter the title to search for: ")
        found_books = [book for book in library if search_title.lower() in book[0].lower()]
        if found_books:
```

```python
        for book in found_books:
            print(f"Title: {book[0]}, Author: {book[1]}")
    else:
        print("No books found with that title.")

    # Exiting the program
    elif action == "exit":
        break

    else:
        print("Invalid action. Please try again.")
```

Explanation:

- The program uses a while loop to continuously offer menu options to the user.
- Each book is stored as a list within the `library` list, creating a nested list structure.
- Users can add new books, view the entire catalog, or search for books by title.
- The search functionality is case-insensitive and checks for the search term within each book's title.

Mini Project 7 Sample Code:

```python
Python
# Multiplication Table Generator

# User input for the upper limit
limit = int(input("Enter the number limit for the multiplication table: "))

# Generating and printing the multiplication table
for i in range(1, limit + 1):
    for j in range(1, limit + 1):
        print(f"{i} x {j} = {i * j}", end='\t')
    print()  # Newline after each row
```

Explanation:

- The program starts by asking the user for the upper limit of the multiplication table.
- It uses nested `for` loops to iterate over the range and calculate the product of each pair of numbers.
- The `print` function uses `end='\t'` for tab-separated formatting.
- A newline is printed after each row to create a table layout.

Mini Project 8 Sample Code:

```python
Python
# Prime Number Finder

# User input for the upper limit
upper_limit = int(input("Enter the upper limit to find prime numbers: "))

# Function to check if a number is prime
def is_prime(number):
    if number < 2:
        return False
    for i in range(2, number):
        if number % i == 0:
            return False
    return True

# Finding and displaying prime numbers
print("Prime numbers:")
for num in range(2, upper_limit + 1):
    if num > 2 and num % 2 == 0:
        continue  # Skip even numbers
    if is_prime(num):
        print(num, end=' ')
```

Explanation:
- The program asks for the upper limit for prime numbers.
- A function `is_prime` is defined to check if a number is prime.
- A `for` loop iterates over the range, using `continue` to skip even numbers for efficiency.
- The program prints each prime number found within the specified limit.

Mini Project 9 Sample Code:

```Python
# Unit Converter: Kilometers and Miles

def km_to_miles(km):
    return km * 0.621371

def miles_to_km(miles):
    return miles / 0.621371

# User interaction for conversion choice
print("Unit Converter - Kilometers and Miles")
choice = input("Convert to (Miles/Km): ").lower()
value = float(input("Enter the value: "))

# Processing and output
if choice == "miles":
    converted = km_to_miles(value)
    print(f"{value} kilometers is {converted} miles.")
elif choice == "km":
    converted = miles_to_km(value)
    print(f"{value} miles is {converted} kilometers.")
else:
    print("Invalid choice.")
```

Explanation:
- Two functions `km_to_miles` and `miles_to_km` are defined for conversions.
- The user is asked to choose the conversion type and enter a value.
- The program then calls the appropriate function and displays the result.

Mini Project 10 Sample Code:

```python
Python
# Simple Calculator with Memory

last_operation = None

def add(a, b):
    return a + b

def subtract(a, b):
    return a - b

def multiply(a, b):
    return a * b

def divide(a, b):
    if b == 0:
        return "Error: Division by zero."
    return a / b

def show_last_operation():
    if last_operation:
        print("Last operation performed:", last_operation)
    else:
        print("No operations performed yet.")

# User interaction loop
while True:
    print("\nSimple Calculator")
    print("1. Add\n2. Subtract\n3. Multiply\n4. Divide\n5. Show Last Operation\n6.
Exit")
```

```python
choice = input("Choose an option: ")

if choice == "6":
    break

if choice in ["1", "2", "3", "4"]:
    num1 = float(input("Enter first number: "))
    num2 = float(input("Enter second number: "))

if choice == "1":
    result = add(num1, num2)
    last_operation = f"Add: {num1} + {num2} = {result}"
elif choice == "2":
    result = subtract(num1, num2)
    last_operation = f"Subtract: {num1} - {num2} = {result}"
elif choice == "3":
    result = multiply(num1, num2)
    last_operation = f"Multiply: {num1} * {num2} = {result}"
elif choice == "4":
    result = divide(num1, num2)
    last_operation = f"Divide: {num1} / {num2} = {result}"
elif choice == "5":
    show_last_operation()
    continue
else:
    print("Invalid option. Please try again.")
    continue

print("Result:", result)
```

Explanation:

- Functions for basic arithmetic operations and showing the last operation are defined.
- The last_operation variable keeps track of the most recent calculation.
- The user chooses an operation and inputs values, and the result is

displayed.

- The program also allows viewing the last operation.

Mini Project 11 Sample Code:

```python
# Personalized Story Creator

def create_story(name, color, hobby):
    story = ("Once upon a time, there was a person named {}. "
        "Their favorite color was {} and they loved {}. "
        "One day, while engaging in {}, they found a {} colored stone, "
        "which granted them their heart's desire.").format(name, color, hobby, hobby,
color)
    return story

# User input
user_name = input("Enter your name: ")
favorite_color = input("Enter your favorite color: ")
hobby = input("Enter your hobby: ")

# Creating and printing the story
personalized_story = create_story(user_name, favorite_color, hobby)
print("\nYour Personalized Story:\n", personalized_story)
```

Explanation:
- The program uses a function `create_story` to generate a story.
- It asks the user for their name, favorite color, and hobby.
- These details are then formatted into a pre-defined story template and displayed.

Mini Project 12 Sample Code:

```Python
# Palindrome Checker

def is_palindrome(s):
    # Standardizing the string
    standardized_str = s.replace(" ", "").lower()
    # Checking for palindrome
    return standardized_str == standardized_str[::-1]

# User input
user_string = input("Enter a string to check if it's a palindrome: ")

# Palindrome check and output
if is_palindrome(user_string):
    print(f"'{user_string}' is a palindrome!")
else:
    print(f"'{user_string}' is not a palindrome.")
```

Explanation:
- The program defines a function is_palindrome to check for palindromes.
- It standardizes the user's input by removing spaces and converting to lowercase.
- The function then checks if the string is equal to its reverse.
- The result is displayed to the user.

Mini Project 13 Sample Code:

```Python
import datetime

# Personal Event Countdown

# Function to calculate the number of days until the event
def days_until_event(event_date):
    today = datetime.date.today()
    return (event_date - today).days

# User input for event date
year = int(input("Enter the year of the event (YYYY): "))
month = int(input("Enter the month of the event (MM): "))
day = int(input("Enter the day of the event (DD): "))
event_date = datetime.date(year, month, day)

# Calculate days remaining and output
days_remaining = days_until_event(event_date)
print(f"Days until your event: {days_remaining}")
```

Explanation:

- The program uses the datetime module to handle dates.
- It defines a function to calculate the number of days until the event.
- The user inputs the date of their event, which is used to calculate the days remaining.
- The program outputs the countdown to the user's event.

Mini Project 14 Sample Code:

```python
Python
import random


# Random Inspirational Quote Generator

# List of inspirational quotes
quotes = [
    "Believe you can and you're halfway there. - Theodore Roosevelt",
    "The only way to do great work is to love what you do. - Steve Jobs",
    "The future belongs to those who believe in the beauty of their dreams. - Eleanor Roosevelt",
    "It does not matter how slowly you go as long as you do not stop. - Confucius",
    "You are never too old to set another goal or to dream a new dream. - C.S. Lewis"
]

# Randomly select and display a quote
selected_quote = random.choice(quotes)
print("Inspirational Quote of the Day:\n", selected_quote)
```

Explanation:
- The program imports the `random` module.
- A list of inspirational quotes is defined.
- The `random.choice()` function is used to randomly select a quote from the list.
- The program then prints the selected quote.

Mini Project 15 Sample Code:

```python
# Personal Contact Book

contact_book = {}

def add_contact(name, phone, email):
    contact_book[name] = {"Phone": phone, "Email": email}

def remove_contact(name):
    if name in contact_book:
        del contact_book[name]
    else:
        print("Contact not found.")

def search_contact(name):
    return contact_book.get(name, "Contact not found.")

# User interaction loop
while True:
    print("\n--- Personal Contact Book ---")
    print("1. Add Contact\n2. Remove Contact\n3. Search Contact\n4. Exit")
    choice = input("Choose an option: ")

    if choice == "1":
        name = input("Enter name: ")
        phone = input("Enter phone number: ")
        email = input("Enter email address: ")
        add_contact(name, phone, email)
        print(f"Contact '{name}' added successfully.")
    elif choice == "2":
```

```
    name = input("Enter name to remove: ")
    remove_contact(name)
    print(f"Contact '{name}' removed successfully.")
elif choice == "3":
    name = input("Enter name to search: ")
    print(search_contact(name))
elif choice == "4":
    break
else:
    print("Invalid option. Please try again.")
```

Explanation:

- The program uses a dictionary to store contact details.
- Functions for adding, removing, and searching contacts are defined.
- The user interacts through a menu to manage the contact book.

Mini Project 16 Sample Code:

```python
# Vocabulary Builder

vocabulary = {}

def add_word(word, meaning):
    vocabulary[word] = meaning

def view_all_words():
    for word, meaning in vocabulary.items():
        print(f"{word}: {meaning}")

def search_word(word):
    return vocabulary.get(word, "Word not found.")

# User interaction loop
while True:
    print("\n--- Vocabulary Builder ---")
    print("1. Add Word\n2. View All Words\n3. Search Word\n4. Exit")
    choice = input("Choose an option: ")

    if choice == "1":
        word = input("Enter word: ")
        meaning = input("Enter meaning: ")
        add_word(word, meaning)
        print(f"Word '{word}' added successfully.")
    elif choice == "2":
        view_all_words()
    elif choice == "3":
        word = input("Enter word to search: ")
        print(search_word(word))
```

```
elif choice == "4":
    break
else:
    print("Invalid option. Please try again.")
```

Explanation:

- The program uses a dictionary to store words and their meanings.
- Functions for adding words, viewing all words, and searching for words are provided.
- The user can interact with the program through a simple menu to manage their vocabulary.

Mini Project 17 Sample Code

```python
Python
import datetime

# Personal Diary Application

def add_entry():
    with open("diary.txt", "a") as file:
        entry = input("Write your diary entry:\n")
        current_time = datetime.datetime.now().strftime("%Y-%m-%d %H:%M:%S")
        file.write(f"{current_time}\n{entry}\n\n")

def view_entries():
    try:
        with open("diary.txt", "r") as file:
            print(file.read())
    except FileNotFoundError:
        print("No diary entries found.")

# User interaction loop
while True:
    print("\n--- Personal Diary ---")
    print("1. Add Entry\n2. View Entries\n3. Exit")
    choice = input("Choose an option: ")

    if choice == "1":
        add_entry()
    elif choice == "2":
        view_entries()
    elif choice == "3":
        break



    else:
        print("Invalid option. Please try again.")
```

Explanation:

- The program allows users to add new diary entries, which include the current date and time.
- Users can also view all their past entries.
- Diary entries are saved to and read from a file named `diary.txt`.

Mini Project 18 Sample Code:

```python
Python
import json

# Contact List Manager

def load_contacts():
    try:
        with open("contacts.json", "r") as file:
            return json.load(file)
    except FileNotFoundError:
        return {}

def save_contacts(contacts):
    with open("contacts.json", "w") as file:
        json.dump(contacts, file, indent=4)

def add_update_contact(contacts):
    name = input("Enter contact name: ")
    phone = input("Enter contact phone: ")
    email = input("Enter contact email: ")
    contacts[name] = {"Phone": phone, "Email": email}

def view_contacts(contacts):
    for name, details in contacts.items():
        print(f"{name} - Phone: {details['Phone']}, Email: {details['Email']}")

# Load contacts from file
contacts = load_contacts()

# User interaction loop
while True:
```

```
print("\n--- Contact List Manager ---")
print("1. Add/Update Contact\n2. View Contacts\n3. Exit")
choice = input("Choose an option: ")

if choice == "1":
    add_update_contact(contacts)
    save_contacts(contacts)
elif choice == "2":
    view_contacts(contacts)
elif choice == "3":
    break
else:
    print("Invalid option. Please try again.")
```

Explanation:

- The program uses JSON file operations to store and manage a contact list.
- Users can add or update contacts, which are then saved to contacts.json
- The load_contacts function loads existing contacts from the file when the program starts.
- Users can view all saved contacts through a simple menu interface.

Mini Project 19 Sample Code:

```python
Python
# Simple Bank Account Manager

class BankAccount:
    def __init__(self, name, initial_balance=0):
        self.name = name
        self.balance = initial_balance

    def deposit(self, amount):
        self.balance += amount
        return self.balance

    def withdraw(self, amount):
        if amount > self.balance:
            return "Insufficient balance"
        self.balance -= amount
        return self.balance

    def check_balance(self):
        return self.balance

# Creating an account
name = input("Enter your name to create a bank account: ")
account = BankAccount(name)

# User interaction loop
while True:
    print("\n--- Bank Account Manager ---")
    print("1. Deposit\n2. Withdraw\n3. Check Balance\n4. Exit")
    choice = input("Choose an option: ")
```

```python
if choice == "1":
    amount = float(input("Enter amount to deposit: "))
    account.deposit(amount)
elif choice == "2":
    amount = float(input("Enter amount to withdraw: "))
    print(account.withdraw(amount))
elif choice == "3":
    print("Current balance:", account.check_balance())
elif choice == "4":
    break
else:
    print("Invalid option. Please try again.")
```

Explanation:

- A `BankAccount` class is defined with methods for deposit, withdraw, and check balance.
- An account object is created for the user.
- The user interacts with the account through a menu-driven interface.

Mini Project 20 Sample Code:

```python
Python
# Library Management System

class Book:
    def __init__(self, title, author):
        self.title = title
        self.author = author

    def __repr__(self):
        return f"'{self.title}' by {self.author}"

class Library:
    def __init__(self):
        self.books = []
        self.borrowed_books = []

    def add_book(self, book):
        self.books.append(book)

    def view_books(self):
        if not self.books:
            print("No books available in the library.")
        else:
            for book in self.books:
                print(book)

    def borrow_book(self, title):
        for book in self.books:
            if book.title == title:
                self.books.remove(book)
```

```python
            self.borrowed_books.append(book)
            return f"You have borrowed {book}"
        return "Book not available"

# Creating a library instance
library = Library()

# User interaction loop
while True:
    print("\n--- Library Management System ---")
    print("1. Add Book\n2. View Books\n3. Borrow Book\n4. Exit")
    choice = input("Choose an option: ")

    if choice == "1":
        title = input("Enter book title: ")
        author = input("Enter book author: ")
        library.add_book(Book(title, author))
        print(f"'{title}' has been added to the library.")
    elif choice == "2":
        library.view_books()
    elif choice == "3":
        title = input("Enter the title of the book you want to borrow: ")
        print(library.borrow_book(title))
    elif choice == "4":
        break
    else:
        print("Invalid option. Please try again.")
```

Explanation:

- The program defines Book and Library classes.
- The Library class has methods to add books, view available books, and borrow books.
- Books are tracked in the library, and borrowed books are moved to a separate list.
- Users interact with the library system through a menu.

ABOUT THE AUTHOR

Jae W. Lee is a dynamic technology business leader and serial entrepreneur with a broad range of experience. He co-founded Kempus, a platform that allows verified students to anonymously exchange reviews about university life and career development without the risk of doxxing. Previously, as the Lead Software Engineer for Cheil Worldwide's UXD team, contributed to user experience design, notably in global digital campaigns for Samsung. His career includes leadership positions at RingMD, a telemedicine service, and Quincus, a logistics platform, where he was the VP of Engineering. Additionally, Jae's innovative spirit shone as the CTO of WorldRoamer, an online agency for booking hotels and activities. For his outstanding contributions to the tech sector, Jae earned a place on the Forbes Technology Council.

www.ingramcontent.com/pod-product-compliance
Lightning Source LLC
La Vergne TN
LVHW052056060326
832903LV00061B/991